T0146876

HITCHHIKING
Across the
ATLANTIC

HITCHHIKING
Across the
ATLANTIC

A SAILING ADVENTURE

Written and Illustrated By:
Lulu Waldron

HITCHHIKING ACROSS THE ATLANTIC
A SAILING ADVENTURE

iUniverse books may be ordered through booksellers or by contacting:

iUniverse
1663 Liberty Drive
Bloomington, IN 47403
www.iuniverse.com
1-800-Authors (1-800-288-4677)

Because of the dynamic nature of the Internet, any web addresses or links contained in this book may have changed since publication and may no longer be valid. The views expressed in this work are solely those of the author and do not necessarily reflect the views of the publisher, and the publisher hereby disclaims any responsibility for them.

Any people depicted in stock imagery provided by Thinkstock are models, and such images are being used for illustrative purposes only. Certain stock imagery © Thinkstock.

ISBN: 978-1-5320-0359-2 (sc)
ISBN: 978-1-5320-0360-8 (e)

Library of Congress Control Number: 2016911984

Print information available on the last page.

iUniverse rev. date: 08/29/2016

Dedicated to my children and grandchildren.
May they have their own exciting and challenging adventures.

Table of Contents

List of Illustrations

Acknowledgment

I thank Selma Beckwith whose gift of editing helped bring this book to life and Teri Brentnall who gave it a final polish. The book cover design is by Jane Sharpe of Jane Sharpe Designs. Austin, Texas. The cover photograph is by Mary Pat Waldron, Studio Penumbre, Austin, Texas. Both are outstanding artists and their contributions to the book cover are truly appreciated.

To the people who helped me out with managing the computer when it got over my head: Mary Pat Waldron and Andrew Levy and to my daughter Dianne for her insights and suggestions.

In grateful appreciation to all my skippers, without whom there would be no journey, and no story.

This is a true story with only the names of boats and people being changed.

Introduction

    Being a person who thrives on challenges I find myself with one of my most difficult ones: trying to share with you my story. It is about a life changing adventure which had so many unplanned twists, that all I could do was keep going and see what God had in store for me. I am compelled to write it down because I think the story needs telling for future generations of my own family and perhaps others who dream of the chance to have a grand adventure. It is my way of encouraging you to get out on the skinny branches of life where you have to face down your fears, celebrate the joy it brings when you do and trust in God's plan for you.

Prolgue

It was late May, 1988 and I was onboard the *Panther*, a 44 foot sailboat. Seventeen days before, Conover, my skipper, and I had set sail from Bermuda for the Azores, a small group of islands approximately 1,900 miles off of the east coast of Portugal. We were nearing our destination and as I took my turn at the night watch, I could see the lights of the island of Faial beckoning to me in the darkness. As much as these lights were summoning me onward, so was the life of adventure that I had, with great trepidation, chosen to pursue. I had joined the ranks of sailors who hitchhiked the oceans of the world by crewing on different boats. Mostly, these sailors were strong, young men and the fact that I was a fifty-five year old grandmother made me a bit of an oddity.

I have come to believe that God had given me this gift of time at sea to teach me to let go, to trust his plan for me, that no matter how hard I tried, or what sacrifices I would make, there were things I could not control. Also that it was okay to try something challenging and, perhaps, fail. That sometimes God closes doors because it's time to move forward and he knows you won't move unless circumstances force you. In the best of all worlds, my journey might have been all on one boat and with people I knew and trusted but, in reality, I had several skippers who treated me in such a way that I had finally learned how and when "to get off the boat". I overcame my fear of what might lie ahead and moved on into a world of uncertainty.

"Never give up on what you really want to do. The person with big dreams is more powerful than one with all the facts."

Albert Einstein

"Be fearless and undaunted, for go where you may, Yahweh your God is with you."

Josh 1:9

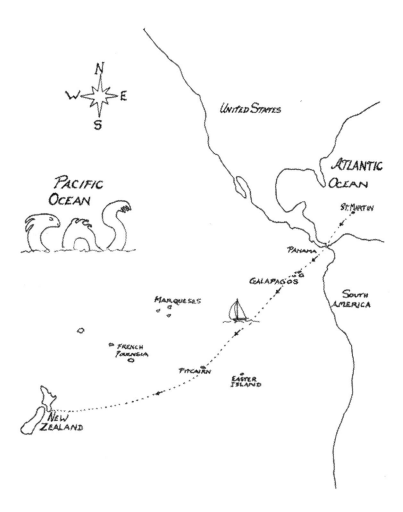

Map of the originally planned six month journey
through the Panama Canal to New Zealand.

The Island Of St Martin

It had all started the end of March, 1988 when I flew from Seattle, Washington to the island of St. Martin in the Caribbean. My friend Peggy and her boyfriend, Don, were planning to sail his 40-foot boat, *Osprey*, through the Panama Canal and then on to the Galapagos and other islands en route to New Zealand. The voyage on which I was invited to crew was to take six months. Although I had been sailing since college, when I was on the sailing team at George Washington University, most of my experience was on rivers, lakes and bays. I had little ocean cruising experience but had always dreamed of a high seas adventure.

The timing of the invitation was perfect for I was feeling very much like a displaced person, confused and very fearful. My marriage of thirty-two years had fallen apart and the pain was indescribable. In spite of my desperate efforts to hold my marriage together, in the end it had failed. Now my dream home overlooking Lake Washington had been sold, my belongings were in storage and my three adult daughters were living their own lives. I felt that this incredible trip that was being offered to me was a lifeline, for I truly didn't know where to turn next.

Osprey had been in dry dock at Bobby's Marina on St. Martin island for several years. Don had flown down some weeks earlier to launch her and get her in shape for the trip ahead. I barely knew Don, but was good friends with his girlfriend, Peggy. I had met Peggy in Seattle, while skiing at Snoqualmie Pass, where she was a member of the Ski Patrol. Peggy had become a bright spot in my life. Being married to a workaholic, I had time to spare, so besides skiing together, Peggy and I had sailed a small boat that she owned. It was fun having a friend who liked to do the same things I did. Then, too, I admired her for raising three wonderful young men, as a single mother. Peggy was tall and slender with almost masculine features. I liked the idea that Don looked beyond her physical looks and saw the wonderful inner person. Don had only recently become part of Peggy's life and agreed to take me on as crew at her request. Our only meeting was in Seattle when he interviewed me regarding my sailing experience.

It was evening in St. Martin when Peggy and I arrived from Seattle. We were among the last people to get through customs, probably because of the eighteen boxes of provisions Peggy had felt were necessary for our six month journey. We were almost through when a customs official decided that I had to have an airline ticket to show I had a way to leave the country. St Martin is a two nation island, half French, half Dutch and neither country wants visitors who might become liabilities. Don was right there to attest to the fact that I would be leaving the Island on his boat, but to no avail. I ran to a ticket counter which was just closing and managed to purchase a ticket to nearby St. Thomas, one of the U.S. Virgin Islands. After finally getting through customs, we discovered that the one remaining taxi, a large van, had just been hired by a young couple. Most kindly, they made room for us and our 18 boxes. We were driven across the island and dropped off at the dock in the town of Philipsburg on Great Bay, located on the Dutch side of the island.

Osprey was anchored well out in the bay and it was now very dark. Don had left his dinghy on the beach and it took many trips, rowing the little wooden boat back and forth, to get all the boxes from the beach to the sailboat. After the first trip, Peggy remained aboard to stow the boxes away; Don did the transporting and I stood guard over the remaining boxes on the dock. This gave me the solitude to absorb my surroundings. It was a truly beautiful evening; the sky was sparkling with a multitude of stars and the reflection of lights from the boats in the harbor danced on the water, so you could hardly tell where the sky stopped and the water began. I felt blessed and also surprised by the joy of realizing a new freedom from my possessions and from my marriage, but mostly elated at the thought of the adventure that lay ahead. I appreciated this time to think and just be. Back in the states, the Hubble Space Telescope was being launched, postage stamps cost

24 cents and Paul Simon's "Graceland" was number one on the music chart. It was also the year crack cocaine hit the market and a bomb exploded on a Pan Am jet over Lockerbie, Scotland. I was very happy to leave that all behind me.

With each trip, we loaded the little dinghy with so many boxes that it looked as if it might sink. As Don rowed off into the night, I wondered where he was heading as I could see no lights of a sailboat. Many trips later he had room for me to go along with the few remaining boxes. I had assumed his sailboat, like most others, would have electric lights; not so, it was totally dark. This was one of many preconceived ideas I had about the *Osprey* that proved to be really wrong.

We finally got all the boxes stacked on deck when, very late at night, it began to rain. There was much confusion as we stumbled around in the dark trying to cram some of the now very soggy boxes below deck and drape a sail over the rest. Finally a lull in the rain allowed us to fall into, what ultimately proved to be, a fitful sleep as it was always interrupted by Don who leapt up every so often to check on things.

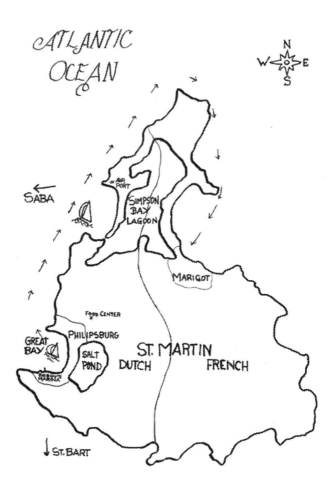

Map of island of St Martin

In the morning it had begun raining again. This was not the paradise I had been anticipating. We tried to jam the remaining boxes into the cabin, before the rain soaked through the sail covering them but, as in the cabin of any boat, most of the space was already occupied by something else. At the end of the day, we had made only a small dent in stowing our supplies. It took us many days trying to find space for all the food Peggy had brought.

Life Aboard Osprey

Right after I moved aboard *Osprey,* Don took me aside to explain a rule he had: a rule just for me. He explained that if I used any of the equipment on the boat in the wrong way (which meant any way Don might disapprove of), that equipment would thereafter be off limits to me. Not an auspicious start for our relationship. One of the oddities about the boat was that there was no kitchen, or in nautical terms, galley. Don had placed a propane stove in the cockpit on deck and it was there that he planned for us to do our cooking. As we set about fixing our meal the next evening, I tried to be helpful by lighting the stove—but it had an intricate starting mechanism and I did it wrong. The ire of Don descended on me like a Caribbean storm. He informed me I could no longer use the stove. He had not thought this through very well, as of course this meant that I would not have to cook. Maybe no one wanted to cook, because from then on we started taking our main meal of the day ashore.

There were other things about *Osprey* that I had amazingly managed to overlook. Like Little Susie Sunshine, I had seen only the bright side of this adventure. My long held dream was about to be fulfilled and I would sail around the world, or a least as far as New Zealand. However, blinded by my great desire to make this journey, I had barely noticed some rather important things. There was no radio, no navigational aids and no bathroom or, in sailing lingo, "head." With regard to the head, according to the publication "Navy Traditions and Customs," the head refers to the bow or forepart of the ship. In the old days a vessel's toilet was placed at the head of the ship near the base of the bowsprit, where splashing water served to naturally clean the toilet area. On *Osprey,* the head was a rubber bucket and that is what we used. There was no holding tank, as on other boats, and it made me really think twice about swimming off the boat! Since there was no head or galley, the interior of the boat was rather roomy, all one open space with a double bed curtained off as the captains quarters and a smaller bed, also curtained off, for the crew. There was a table and chairs in the center and cabinets built in around the walls. There was a large storage space in the bow of the boat and that is where we eventually stored all the food.

Another major item missing from *Osprey* was a motor. A motor would enable us to get into places that we could not manage under sail, but even more importantly, it would also recharge batteries. Don wanted to use solar for his energy source and it was not working; at night we lived mostly in the dark. Living in the moment as I was, I had not envisioned how we would manage at sea, where we would have none of the amenities we were getting used to ashore, like eating at restaurants and using pay showers at the marina. Eventually I began to visualize us out in the middle of the ocean, cooking on deck in good weather and bad, using our bucket /head when the seas were rough, never having a proper bath for six months, not being able to radio for help when personalities and circumstances conspired in our trying to kill each other.

Osprey was made of cement. Don had built her some years earlier and decided at that time it was safer to not put any holes in the boat for things like a motor, a head or a galley. I understood his reasoning on this, for now there would be no possibility of water leaking in. But why no radio or navigational equipment? Being hand-built by Don helped explained the very odd configuration of the interior of the boat, like nothing I had ever seen. *Osprey* was steered by a long tiller and had two sets of sails. The original set was of heavy canvas, the color of weak tea. In Seattle, Don had ordered some new, light-weight sails for the trip. When I saw the name Hasse on them, I felt like a friend had come along. I had met Carol Hasse in Seattle and was aware she was making quite a name for herself as a sailmaker in the Puget Sound area.

In appearance Don was short and trim, with only a slight paunch to show for his 55 years. His lower face was covered with a short beard and his hair was cut in a conventional manner but he wore two earrings in his right ear. I wondered if Don's boat was a refection of his personality, rigid and unconventional. Perhaps I should have, but I never questioned his competence. He had sailed down the eastern seaboard and eventually to St. Martin and that was good enough for me. It did seem to me, however, that Don had ceased to own the boat, if indeed he ever had. Truly *Osprey* owned him. Her safety and care came before all other considerations. She was always anchored well out in the harbor, away from other boats and he secured all hatches and portholes with large locks.

There was only one way to do things on Don's boat, even the simplest thing like drawing up a bucket of seawater or lighting the stove, and that was Don's way. This presented a problem when it came to rowing the dinghy. Don was proficient at rowing but because the oars were too long for the little wooden dinghy, the handles overlapped and I was forever bruising my knuckles. I don't know why I always got the job of rowing, but I taught myself to adapt by alternating oars and, for the moment, Don seemed to tolerate my technique. At one point, Don had thought of having us carry the oars with us wherever we went on land—lest someone be tempted to steal the dinghy. Since they were so long and the streets crowded with people and vehicles, he eventually dropped that idea.

The town of Philipsburg had two main streets, Front Street and Back Street, each fifteen or twenty blocks long. A dominant structure on Front Street was the Catholic church, which had a steeple and bell tower. The bells chimed the quarter hours and tolled the hours. They had a lovely sound which carried over the waters of Great Bay. The shops in the little town were duty-free, and early every morning several cruise ships arrived and anchored in the harbor, where people were ferried ashore to shop and explore. By evening, they were gone. Many ships and boats were anchored in the crescent-shaped harbor, including freighters, a U.S. Navy destroyer that was lit up like a Christmas tree every night, and sailboats of every size imaginable. There were even beautiful three and four masted "tall ships," that took on paying passengers.

The bay itself had a sloping bottom so, except in bad weather, most of the water motion was gently rolling waves. When the seas were rough, however, we did experience a great deal of pitching and rolling which was most uncomfortable in the concrete boat. I found I really had to hold on to something for stability and hoped I would not have to use the bucket/head. One such night, we drifted perilously close to another boat. Peggy and I struggled to haul up the heavy anchor, as Don ran a line from *Osprey* to the dinghy. He then rowed and towed the *Osprey* farther out in the bay. At this point I was still too inexperienced to understand the implications the lack of a motor would have once we left port.

Slowly the days slipped by and still we were not ready to depart. Several times Don visited an acquaintance, who had a radio, hoping to get information about getting through the Panama Canal such as the cost and the waiting time to transit. We rowed ashore each day and ate our main meal at Zumi's, a small open-air restaurant on the beach, where delicious vegetarian food was served by the owners, Nancy and Rupert. The service was slow, they called it island-time, but we were not in a hurry. Our only task seemed to be to buy more food, which we almost never ate. I found that puzzling but, caught up in my dream, I ignored this curiosity.

Our first Sunday in Philipsburg was Easter Sunday, and both Peggy and Don decided to go to church with me. We rowed our dinghy right up onto the sandy beach below the church and made it just in time to find places inside. It was very crowded, with a mixture of people, mostly black locals who lived there and a sprinkling of white yachting people and tourists. The locals looked very handsome dressed in their best clothes. The little boys wore suits and the girls were in frilly dresses, with their hair done in bows. I was glad I had brought a skirt to use for just such an occasion. The church was a wooden structure; the doors were on the sides since the building was located on an extremely busy street. The interior had graceful wooden arches and there were many statues of saints. The mass was said in English, the language used on both sides of the island and I enjoyed the service.

Several days after I had boarded *Osprey* and received my set of rules, Don had given me a 2-foot length of rope to test my knot tying skills. It seemed that I had gone through life without learning all my nautical knots and I flunked the test. The most difficult for me was the bowline, which one is supposed to be able to remember with the help of a little ditty. It was something about the rope, represented by a rabbit which would go around a tree and down a hole, but I never got it right ——getting the rabbit and the tree, and sometimes myself, confused. Furthermore, I felt strongly that the Don should call the rope a line. In my sailing experience, I would have asked someone to toss me a line. No matter; since I had failed the test, Don issued another rule: I was required to carry the rope [or line] with me at all times, so I could practice for my next test. Like he did on most evenings, Easter Sunday evening Don sat me down for a fault-finding session and he scolded me roundly for not taking the rope with me to church. First the stove and now the rope, I realized that if I did not do better Don would put me ashore. That thought was very frighting and I would do anything to not let that happen. I would have to try harder to do everything right and get Don to like me. At this point I was feeling very lonely and isolated, I had so counted on this trip. The rope was my closest friend from then on.

Peggy and I spent most of our days shopping for food to add to the eighteen boxes of provisions we had brought with us from Seattle. There was a small bus system in Philipsburg that consisted of minivans, driven by enterprising individuals who hand-lettered their destinations on the sides of their vehicles. We found one that we could flag down and used it to get back and forth for our almost daily trip to the grocery store, located some miles away. One day after shopping, we had quite a large number of bags and there was no bus to take us back to Philipsburg. We saw two men going to a car, who also had bags of groceries. They looked like they might be boating types, so we felt safe in asking them for a ride. They were very kind and not only gave us a ride but drove us right onto the beach and helped us load our dinghy. In the days ahead they became good friends and proved to be a huge blessing to me.

The Parasail Boat

Our new friends were from Utah, although the older man, Jim, was originally from Australia. They were in St. Martin starting a parasail business. Jim's younger companion, Nick, a handsome young man, was newly married and he and his beautiful wife Louise, Mormon missionaries, were earning a living by helping Jim start the business. Jim was a great big man with a great big heart. His clothing set him apart, for he always had on white coveralls and a white Aussie hat with the brim turned up on one side. The hat had an insignia showing a small dog watching a box, bearing the words "Tucker Box." If you were willing to take the time, Jim would tell you a yarn about the insignia, and if yarns were gold Jim would have been a very wealthy man. He never ran out of stories or happy boisterous songs. He loved to get people singing and accompanied them on his harmonica. In the days that followed, the three of them often motored over in their boat and gave me a ride in the parasail over Great Bay and other bays nearby where a few hotels were located. My job was to wave to the land lubbers and be a flying advertisement. Such a lovely job.

Although they tried to include Don and Peggy, Don showed no interest in their friendship and in fact actually shunned them. Peggy always chose to stay with Don, even though I could tell she would really have liked to join us. She never criticized Don, at least not out loud, but the take-charge, fun loving person I had so admired seemed to be disappearing. It didn't occur to me to ask her how she felt, or if she tired of having to complete the never-ending list of chores that filled her days. Having lived with domineering men in my past, I understood her choices and once would have behaved in the same way. My father had ruled our family absolutely, and as children, we had learned not to question. And then—I didn't realize it at the time—I married a man in some ways similar to my father.

As I look back on the events that followed, I realize it was all part of Don's plan, how to get Lulu off the boat or "Operation Lose Lulu." He had taken me on as crew at the request of his girl friend and it was not working out to his satisfaction. Now he hoped that if he made my life difficult enough, I would leave voluntarily; but I was like a barnacle clinging to an old wooden boat. Rejection and criticism were negatives I had grown accustomed to and had learned to ignore; not that they didn't hurt, but I just kept on keeping on. This conditioning had allowed me to ignore Don's behavior thus far. However his next ploy almost got me. He starting strutting around the deck in his altogether. That is to say he was naked as a bluejay. This was a first for me, as I had led quite a sheltered life. Inside I was truly and deeply shocked. At first I acted like I didn't see him, but round and round the deck he went, until I could no longer pretend. When we sat down that night for one of the talks, wherein he informed me of some new fault he had found in me, he was most upset that I did not mention his nakedness. What did he expect me to say, that I had seen better? Alas I had to keep mum on that subject as I didn't want to be put ashore. Don's plan to get rid of me was definitely escalating, but so was my determination to persevere. Leave and do what? Go where? Not back to Seattle. I just had to hang in there.

Jim, the Aussie, and I enjoyed each other's company and he often motored over in his boat to pick me up so we could do things together. Sometimes we'd go to Nick and Louise's little apartment, where I could enjoy the luxury of a hot shower and we'd sit around and eat pizza. Sometimes we'd just walk down Front Street and find a little bar where I'd order beer and Jim, being a Mormon, ordered a non alcoholic beverage. Don was probably happy to have me gone for the evening and as I was not there to receive any new rules (a rare treat), we were both happy. One night when I returned quite late, Jim pulled up beside *Osprey* so I could climb aboard. Thinking I had made the transition from one boat to the other, Jim pulled away too soon only to see me fall into the drink. He was horrified, but I thought it was funny.

It was a nice night for a swim. Oh! I had forgotten this was where we dumped the bucket/head. Climbing quickly aboard *Osprey*, I tried to keep from laughing, so as not to wake Simon Legree, who would make a rule that no laughing was allowed.

Sailing To The French Side

After several weeks, Don decided to set sail for a trip part way around the island, from the Dutch side to the French side. Peggy and I pulled up the heavy, rusty anchor, and with a following sea, we sailed a broad reach around the coast line to Marigot. What a treat it was to finally be at sea, even if it was only for a couple of hours! The harbor on the French side was beautiful, more exposed and open, but calmer, without the rolling motion of Great Bay. It was full of boats at anchor, most of them large, well appointed sailboats. It had quite a different feel from the harbor on the Dutch side, as there were no commercial vessels of any kind. The people we saw coming ashore were most often French families. One very large rubber dinghy was loaded with three children, their parents, a baby buggy, a bicycle and a dog. Another delightful sight was a skipper steering his large yacht by moving the wheel with one hand, while cradling his infant in the other. I wanted to be on one of those boats, where people were happy and having fun; but I didn't have the courage to leave the boat I was on.

We dropped anchor, rowed ashore and for the next few days we enjoyed exploring, eating delicious food at small restaurants, and looking in the elegant shops. Marigot was quite a bit larger than Philipsburg and prosperous looking with lovely, stucco homes of pink, yellow and pale blue. The Catholic church was a simple wooden structure, with shutters for the windows, which otherwise would have been open to the elements.

On one of our trips ashore, Don had told me that I was not rowing the dinghy properly and must pull both oars at the same time. Just previous to this, he had informed me that I was not to go on deck without another person, i.e. Peggy. So, I was back to squashed fingers and, for the most part, confined to the cabin. I realized, at last, that this was intolerable. Once we were at sea, I would be trapped. There would be no help from Peggy, who was becoming ever more subservient to Don.

It was not difficult for me to leave, once I had made the decision. Everything I had brought with me would fit in my large duffel bag. My family thought I was crazy to make this trip and had given me whatever they could think of to help make the journey safer. My son-in-law, Bob, an experienced sailor, had given me a safety harness so as to attach myself to a lifeline on the boat. This was for use when I was alone on watch at night. He had also given me a pair of size small foul weather pants, since he knew gear provided on a boat would be too big. My daughter, Teri, who is a doctor, had assembled quite an assortment of medical supplies she felt I might need in an emergency on the six month journey to New Zealand. She had included medications for pain, diarrhea, skin infections, heart attack, lacerations, even toothaches. There were sheets of instructions for treating broken appendages, concussions, (I think she thought I would be climbing the mast and would fall), for wounds, for heart-attacks, and various other contingencies. I packed them all; I was not leaving any of them for Don. I decided it would be good for him to experience some of these misfortunes without my help. I was also taking my bag of wonderful, sweet lemons picked from a tree in Teri and Bob's backyard in California. Let Captain Bligh get scurvy without me. My clothing, bedding and towels were crammed into my bag, along with one other item to which I had given a great deal of thought. In addition to my sailing skills, might a skipper have any expectations of me, as a woman? I had packed my large, white "New Jerusalem Bible", which I planned to place on my chest when it was my turn to sleep. In any case, I never had a problem.

It had taken him quite a little time, but Don's plan to have me leave of my own volition had worked. Peggy did not have much to say, as it was my choice to leave and her choice to stay with Don. Possibly she felt helpless to change anything, for she was no longer the person with whom I had started the journey. When we all sat down to talk about my decision to leave, Don and Peggy showed no surprise. They probably wondered why it had taken me so long.

They hadn't counted on my fear of the unknown, that had kept me trapped. We discussed my contribution to the food costs for the journey and Don came up with a rough estimate for a refund, which he gave to me. It felt as if they had already talked about, and probably planned for, this outcome. Peggy accompanied me on the ride back to Philipsburg where she left me. In spite of everything I felt we parted friends.

Finding A New Boat

During the time *Osprey* had been at anchor in Great Bay, we had rowed the dinghy ashore daily and pulled it up on the sandy beach near Bobby's Marina. One day, while exploring what the marina had to offer in the way of facilities, I had noticed a board containing ads and personal messages. It was a crude affair, tacked up on the wall of the marina office. I had perused it, mostly out of needing something to do while I waited my turn to call home from the U.S. Direct phone booth, where I could use my AT&T card. There were quite a few notices from both power and sail boats, looking for crew. One had been posted by two girls. They admitted they didn't have much sailing experience, but claimed they looked good in their bikinis and were very tan. I remember thinking at the time, that I did have sailing experience and I could pay my own way. But it was early on in the trip; I already had a crewing job and never dreamed that I would need to use that board. One notice particularly stayed in my mind: "Shy skipper who is lonely would like crew to keep company on yacht *Jollymore*." That was so sad, I wondered who would answer such an ad.

It was these notices that came to mind on the ride back to Philipsburg. Should I try to find another boat on which to crew? Hitchhiking on different boats with totally unknown skippers would have once been way out of my comfort zone. But now? What now? Should I give up and fly back to Seattle? Should I start eating the lemons? Trying to make lemonade had certainly been a flop.

The fact that I had nowhere to stay became a strong incentive to act; so I forced myself to get out of my comfort zone and contact various skippers who had notices posted on the board. My other alternative was to sleep outside, under one of the boats sitting in dry dock. That idea was not original with me, I had met a man

16

doing just that. We met one day when I came ashore and he was sitting nearby on a grassy bank, holding a shirt up to dry in the sun after a rainy night. Striking up a conversation with this man, who seemed to have nothing to do but dry his shirt, I learned he was on the lam from the IRS. He looked to be in his forties and might have been executive material in his past life. The thing that struck me was the sparkle in his eyes, maybe he had discovered one of the ways to true happiness, own next to nothing. Checking out all the notices, I came to a dead end. Some boats were heading back to the states; not an option. Others, upon contacting the skippers, said that they had already filled the position—which was shorthand for "You're not what we are looking for." The sad ad, the one posted by the shy, lonely skipper of the *Jollymore* was no longer on the board, but as I walked the docks, chatting with people to see if they had any leads, I met him! He had become discouraged by the lack of response and had taken down the ad. So now I knew: I was the sort of person who would answer such an ad. The skipper's name was Albert and he was bound for Venezuela. It was so amazing that I had just run across him like that; perhaps this was what I was meant to do. We discussed his destination, financial arrangements and what my duties would be and so it was decided: I boarded *Jollymore*, a 30-foot Olson sailboat, beautifully designed for both cruising and racing.

Life Aboard Jollymore

With joy I noted that the boat had a head, a motor, a radio, a tiny galley with a small two burner propane stove, and an inflatable dinghy with a small motor. It even had a small TV. As an added bonus, there were two hand-held radios which Albert and I could use for communicating, when one of us went ashore. The cabin was small, with benches which doubled as bunks, on either side of a table. To have some privacy, and to keep us from falling out during rough weather, there was a large piece of canvas under each bunk that could be pulled up and attached by lines to hooks in the ceiling. It was a narrow space, but I found it quite cozy.

My new skipper was short and slender and looked to be in his mid-thirties. He seemed quite reserved or shy, but had a much less serious outlook on life and was amenable to more enjoyable pastimes—such as going ashore for ice cream cones, instead of more groceries. He had a large supply of canned baked beans, his favorite food, and he figured we could buy whatever else we needed at various islands along the way. What a difference it was to be on *Jollymore*, away from the critical eye of Don and the obsessive grocery buying of Peggy. It did occur to me that, for them, needing ever more groceries might be a ploy to avoid leaving; that they might be nervous or even afraid about making the trip. And on a cement boat as ill-equipped as *Osprey*, I now believed they had good reason to be afraid. I don't know why it took me so long to see what a bad situation it was, I think fear was a very large factor: the boat you know about might be better than the next boat you might get on. I also think it was a bad habit, for I had learned to ignore anything that might break-up my marriage. I had gotten very good at ignoring.

My old friends, Jim, Nick and Louise, were happy to include Albert in the their parasail adventures and Jim spent some time explaining how the whole operation worked since Albert had never been up in a parasail. Jim showed how the rider stood on the large back deck of the speedboat, stepped into a wide mesh seat or harness with a strap that went between the legs, and was then clipped to the lines attached to the parasail. As the boat moved forward, the sail filled with air, and the rider was pulled up off the deck. The rider, now clear of the boat, sailed higher and higher into the sky as the boat increased its speed. From up there, it felt like being a bird, a tethered bird. There were great views of the town of Philipsburg, the cone shaped mountains inland, and the many beautiful yachts and cruise ships at anchor. The water was shades of dark and light blue, depending on its depth and whether the bottom was seaweed or sand. Albert was delighted at the opportunity to go aloft and enjoyed it as much as I did.

Some days later Jim wanted to try using a new parasail with Albert and me. We were willing guinea pigs. He had designed what he called a honeymoon sail, which he planned to publicize as a romantic way for a couple to go up together. He even envisioned a minister standing on the deck, saying the marriage vows. I wondered if he expected the minister to use a megaphone to communicate, since it was difficult for a person to hear anything when up in the air. "Hello up there, do you two take each other for better or worse?" Perhaps I was just too old-fashioned.

The new parasail was much larger than the regular one and quite garish: pink with red hearts and lettering saying "Happy Honeymoon". Getting it to fly was quite a challenge; it was barely airborne before the sail was pulled into the sea by a passing wave. It had to be hauled out of the water and the process of straightening the 16 lines that attached the parasail to the harness was repeated. Jim and Louise spent what seemed like an eternity straightening out the lines, while Nick drove the boat slowly into the wind. A second attempt was made and again the parasail dove into the water. All the lines were straight, but this time the parasail was inside out. The third try was successful, so Albert was clipped onto the honeymoon sail and then I was clipped onto it right in front of him. The boat took off and we were gently lifted into the air. It was fun to have someone who could share your delight in flying, but after several minutes it became increasingly uncomfortable to be in harness so close to another person and some modification was definitely needed. For the harness to work properly, it was important to keep your weight on the strap under your seat. However, we were too close together and were slipping slowly into a position where our weight was no longer on our seats, but rather on the strap between our legs and that was all that was holding us. You can imagine how that felt, especially for Albert. We were dying here. We signaled wildly to be brought down while Louise, megaphone in hand, was asking whether we could make it around the next point of land. I was in agony; my muscles, that were keeping me from being split in two, were giving out. Louise finally realized our desperation and they brought us down. Jim clearly needed to redesign the sail and we never saw it again, in the time we were there.

One afternoon Jim decided to teach me to water ski. I seemed to catch on to his coaching and was soon up on the skis. Jim was very proud of the good job he had done instructing me, telling everyone what a great teacher he was. When I started criss-crossing the wake of the boat, he became suspicious that I was not new to this sport and he was right. My punishment was a thorough dunking,

Albert and I had really been enjoying St. Martin with our parasailing and water skiing. We had even taken Jim, Nick and Louise with us for an afternoon sail to the near by island of Anguilla, where we swam ashore and walked on a lovely, pristine beach. Two weeks had passed very quickly, we were having such fun. However, Albert felt it was time to move on if we wanted to get to Antigua, our first destination, in time to be part of an event called Race Week. Motoring to the Texaco dock, we filled up with fuel and fresh water, then went ashore to have our passports stamped. I made a phone call from the U.S. Direct phone booth to let my children know of my new plans and gave them an address to reach me at the post office in Antigua, where we planned to spend some time. It was hard saying goodbye to our dear friends in St. Martin. They had helped me endure the time I spent on *Osprey,* when I truly needed friends. They had been incredibly kind to me. As we sailed out of the harbor, we kept our sights set on our first landmark ahead, Saba, an island formed from the cone of a volcano.

Leaving St. Martin

I had begun to discover that Albert had certain rituals that were important to him. For instance, on the first night at sea, he liked to eat a big dinner. Under his direction, using a pressure cooker, I prepared a meal of corned beef, potatoes, and mixed vegetables. As I served up the plates, it became obvious that I had missed something along the way—for Albert was truly disappointed at not having baked beans added to the concoction. The volume of food he ate took me by surprise, as he was quite slender. He polished off all the food and I wondered where he would have put a can of baked beans. I washed the dishes in a bucket of sea water and began thinking about turning in, while Albert stood watch. As darkness fell, there was a full moon that shone with a special brilliance in the star-filled sky. The moonlight dancing on the water revealed the silhouette of Saba in the distance behind us. That helped to show the progress we were making.

The gentle, rocking motion of the boat was wonderful for sleeping and before I knew it, it was midnight and time for my watch. Albert instructed me on what compass heading to keep and cautioned me to look out for ships. We had left Saba far behind and could barely see the outline of what we believed to be the island of St. Christopher, or better known as St. Kitts, ahead and to our starboard. Albert turned in after telling me to call him if I had any problems. For a while I really enjoyed my watch, but as the island ahead never seemed to get any closer and there were no other ships visible, I found I was having trouble staying awake. At dawn Albert took over and was disappointed to find that St Kit's was still ahead and Antigua was nowhere in sight. We continued to make very slow progress and, after several more hours, Albert decided to sail to an anchorage near St Kitts and wait for better wind. We had only sailed 53 miles. We checked the charts and found a cove where a ship had sunk, that suggested a good snorkeling site and we arrived there about midday. There were four other yachts at anchor in the cove, probably with the same idea. The snorkeling held little of interest, just schools of sand colored fish and purple sea fans. I did learn one thing: another of Albert's rituals. After each trip at sea, Albert liked to sleep for twenty-four hours. Therefore, right after our snorkeling expedition, he headed for his bunk, not to emerge again until morning. That was a mere fifteen hours, but then our planned passage had been greatly abbreviated. The next day there was still no wind, so we turned on the "iron jib" and motored to the nearby island of Nevis, keeping as a visual fix, an aqua colored dome that showed up very well from a distance. It was late morning when we arrived at the capital, Charlestown, which, with its sulfur baths, had once been a famous Caribbean health resort but now was a backwater town.

Any hope of finding a marina with facilities like a shower were dashed; there was nothing but a cement pier. Wearing salty clothes, and bathing in salt water for days on end, dries the skin and makes it slightly itchy. Once, back in Philipsburg, when I was wearing my swimsuit under my clothes in preparation for a parasail ride later in the day, I had discovered the door to the showers at Bobby's Marina had been left open. The shower area was always locked, even though you had to pay a quarter for each two minutes of cold water. I think the door was open because the electricity was off. Since I had my swimsuit on, I could leave the door open for light, while I rinsed away the salt. Ever since, whenever there was a chance of finding fresh water, I was prepared and ever hopeful of another opportunity.

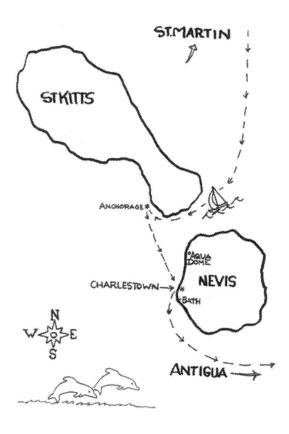

Map of St. Kitts and Nevis

We tied up to the pier and headed for the police station in the square; then to customs, to check in and have our passports stamped. The town was tiny and we decided to walk toward the aqua dome that had guided us in. It turned out to be part of a hotel and I wanted a closer look. By offering to buy drinks, I was able to get Albert to accompany me to the hotel bar. We took our drinks out to the patio, but I did not so much as admire the view or take a sip of my drink! There before me was a swimming pool of fresh, cool water. Not knowing that I had come prepared, Alberts's jaw dropped as I stripped off my outer clothes and dove in. Ahh, bliss!

The view from poolside was enchanting; a wide strip of beach, a grove of graceful palm trees and no buildings. It was so quiet; it felt as though the island was still in the eighteenth century. One could feel the presence of Alexander Hamilton, who was born here, and of Admiral Lord Nelson, the famous British hero, as he courted and married the beautiful young widow Fanny Nisbet, who had a home here. Nevis is only twenty-six square miles in size and, in the 1800s, was largely comprised of sugar plantations, which were now abandoned and in various states of disrepair. Later in the day, we took time to visit one of the historic homes and found the floor and walls were of marble. Possibly sturdy protection from hurricanes?

By this time, I had discovered Albert ate only one meal a day; the rest of the time he was content with coffee and cigarettes. He explained his eating habits by saying he had been a bus driver in London; as though that fact made sense of everything. That night, we prepared for the rest of our trip to Antigua and ate our send off meal. Albert made sure that this time I included the baked beans. We left Nevis in the wee small hours and passed the islands of Montserrat and Redondo at dawn. I found Montserrat to be a forbidding sight, rising out of the sea like a solid rock mound, with no sign of a beach. It was said that there was a post office on the island, it was hard to figure where it would perch and why it would be there. A jet plane flew overhead, leaving a contrail that caught the light of the rising sun. It looked as though a delicate golden ribbon was being pulled through the sky. By late morning we had drawn near to Antigua, and Albert had gone below to check his charts. I became increasingly aware of a reef dead ahead. I called Albert, but he insisted there was no reef in the area; he said he had checked very carefully and we had already passed the reef. I was looking at waves breaking as they do on a beach, only there was no beach. To me, that meant reef. I became more insistent and, finally, Albert came on deck, took one look and immediately brought the boat around. We backtracked for a bit while Albert, completely undone, took the sails down and then we motored to English Harbor, Antigua.

Map of Antigua

Race Week in Antigua

It was Race Week in Antigua, famous throughout the sailing community, with boats coming from all over the world to compete and join in the festivities. It was the best sailing regatta in the Caribbean and ranked among the finest in the world. Held in late April or early May, it was the last big event before boats left the Caribbean to avoid the hurricane season. It had been Albert's dream to crew on one of the racing boats for the week. Much of what he had learned about sailing and navigating, had been self-taught and he hoped to learn more by being on a boat with more experienced sailors, under racing conditions. Most of the books in Albert's small library were about the skills involved in sailing and navigating, as well as stories of famous sailors. Albert had bought *Jollymore* a few years before, with money inherited from his grandmother, and had done some sailing around the Mediterranean before attempting to cross the Atlantic. He said he had a more experienced couple as crew for that trip and spoke highly of their skills and of how helpful they had been to him. But he also told me that he put them off on an island after some disagreement. This information raised a red flag in my mind. Not again!

As we motored toward English Harbor, Albert complained about the continuing lack of wind and said he was thinking of heading back to England. Next he stated he might paint the boat and do other work aboard *Jollymore* when he got to Antigua, since he had already seen the island and did not care about going ashore. It soon became clear to me that Albert had been seriously shaken by his navigational error. He had lost whatever confidence he had possessed and with it, all anticipation for the races. As we came into the harbor, there were people who recognized Albert from other ports and earlier times. Several called out a welcome and invitations to visit. Albert did not seem happy to see any of them and with the briefest of replies, bordering on being rude, went about the business of finding an anchorage. Once we were anchored, we went ashore to do our check-in routine and tied the dinghy up at Nelson's dockyard. This was where Admiral Horatio Nelson and the British West Indies fleet were home ported during the eighteenth century and it was used for making naval repairs and storing supplies until 1899. The harbor offered superb shelter for boats and the surrounding hills were still dotted with old forts. At Nelson's dockyard, we found historic buildings that had been renovated and were experiencing vibrant new life as bakeries, pubs, restaurants and small hotels, as well as marine support businesses—such as a sail makers, chandlers, grocery stores and an electronic repair facility. A market building contained numerous vendors' stalls for local products, a bank, a post office and a cable and wireless office. There were fresh water showers available, and even a library and an art and picture framing shop. The area was crowded with yachting types and everywhere native vendors were selling T-shirts and trinkets.

We checked in with the police and customs and then I invited Albert for a drink at the near by Admiral's Inn, my treat. This seemed to work pretty well as a bribe to get Albert to have a little fun; on some people I use cookies. He reluctantly agreed and we wandered into a charming old building that had been a sail loft, and was now a hotel with a small lobby, seating area and bar. The floor was brick; very uneven and there were French doors opening onto a veranda which overlooked the harbor. We took our drinks out there to enjoy the breeze and the view.

I realized that Albert would be miserable if he carried out his plan to work on his boat, while everyone else was involved in and excited about the upcoming races. I finally brought up the subject and reminded him that the purpose of our coming to Antigua was to fulfill a dream of his. I talked about the courage it took for him to leave England and cross the Atlantic. I pointed out it's okay to try something and perhaps fail [something I was also learning.] That if you are not willing to take a risk, you will not enjoy success. After another drink, I had persuaded Albert to at least go to the race committee desk, just to see if there were any boats that still needed crew. The races were to start in two days, so there was no time to debate it any longer.

There was indeed a list of yachts: racing, cruising, racing/cruising and multi-hull, all needing additional personnel. Their VFH call letters were included. Albert went through the list and copied off the names of two boats. Both were quite a bit larger than *Jollymore*, but of the same class, racing/cruising. He was definitely in better spirits after taking some action. Perhaps I should become a counselor or maybe a bartender; they seem to go together.

The following morning, Albert radioed one of the boats. The skipper thought they had all the crew they needed, but said to call back in the afternoon just to be sure. He tried the second yacht, *Stormy Weather,* but there was no answer. I became concerned about his growing restlessness and encouraged him to call back later in the morning. He finally reached the skipper of *Stormy Weather,* who invited him to come over at noon—when he would be talking with other prospective crew members. Albert gave me a lift ashore in the dinghy on his way to the interview and we planned to meet at a place called Limey's Bar afterwards.

Limey's was on the second floor of a building that had once been officers' quarters. The lower level was now occupied by a gift shop, an art gallery and bathrooms. On the way there I bought a small meat pie at a nearby bakery, picked up a Red Stripe Beer at the bar, and went to sit at one of the picnic tables on the deck. It was a great location from which to see all the harbor activities. There were yachts tied from one end of the long harbor wall to the other and in the crescent-shaped harbor there were boats of all description from all over the world. It made a lovely display. Falmouth Harbor, less than a half mile away, boasted neither dockyard nor harbor wall, but it was also filled with yachts at anchor, as was the far side of Falmouth Harbor, where the Catamaran Club and the Antigua Yacht Club were located. This was high season for Antigua, no doubt about it.

While sitting at Limey's I met several free-lance journalists who had come to write stories that they hoped would capture the essence of Race Week, and earn them a nice paycheck. I also met Philippa, a young Swedish girl who was crewing on a Canadian boat. It turned out that two of her crew-mates were the others meeting for the interview on *Stormy Weather.* Albert arrived a bit later, looking very pleased. He had been invited to crew on *Stormy Weather,* as had Philippa's crew-mates. They considered themselves lucky because *Stormy Weather* had enjoyed quite a name in racing circles, ever since she had been built in the mid-thirties and was still a hard boat to beat when given a good crew.

A young man by the name of Cal was also a crew member on *Stormy Weather* and Albert had invited him to stay on *Jollymore* for the duration of Race Week. Cal was a short, slightly built twenty-eight year old, who looked much younger. His home was New York City, but he was originally from Cuba. He had been hitchhiking around the Caribbean for several years, sometimes for pay and sometimes not. He had a job on the island of Tortola for a while and had recently gotten off a charter-boat where he had been a paid crew. He had been staying with a young man whom he had met at the dockyard, but who had turned out to be a drug-addict and had gone through Cal's things and stolen his money. Cal had hopes of getting some of his money back, but meantime was totally broke and in need of a job as paid crew.

The next morning, the first day of racing, Albert and Cal got up early for they were anxious to get going. Albert had his usual coffee and cigarettes but Cal looked to me like he had not eaten in some time, so I persuaded him to share my granola and milk. The milk was from a carton that didn't have to be refrigerated until it was opened, ideal for a small boat. I found I could keep it cool for a few days, if I wrapped it in a wet cloth.

At precisely 7:30, we motored over in the dinghy to *Stormy Weather.* I wished them good luck, bon voyage, fair winds and following seas, and they climbed aboard. I planned to watch the end of the race from Fort Buchanan, atop one of the surrounding hills. That would not be until late afternoon, however, and there was no way I could see any of the earlier part of the race. But that was all right; I found, as I headed back to *Jollymore*, that race or no race, I was looking forward to having time to myself.

My first priority was exercise: I had been doing too much sitting around. I decided on a good, long swim but stayed in the harbor and swam around anchored boats until I was pleasantly tired. Then, I did laundry by washing and then rinsing my clothes in a bucket of salt water. To the last rinse, I added one eighth cup of Amway fabric softener. This trick, which I learned from reading a book about cruising, got most of the salt out so that the clothes would dry. Next, I used a device Albert had made after seeing it on another boat. It was a large canister of fresh water equipped with a hose, nozzle and a pump to get air pressure into the canister. It had been designed to spray plants with insecticide, but worked great as a fresh water shower and I happily used it on myself.

Map of The First Race

Motoring ashore later in the day, I tied the dinghy up to a seawall near Fort Buchanan. Climbing a steep path, I reached a crumbling fort with an old brass canon on display. From this spot, I had a view of the harbor entrance and was able to see the last leg of the race. *Stormy Weather* won—I was sure of it, but I still wanted to get down to hear if it was official and join the celebration.

As I picked my way down the path I felt so blessed. It was all working out. My turbulent childhood, my stern and unapproachable father, being part of a constantly relocating military family as a Army brat, my marriage to a domineering military man, all difficult for many years but all part of the person I was becoming. I had learned flexibility and finally was learning self-reliance. It had always been part of my nature to challenge myself, as I had done by undertaking this voyage; and had I not found the courage to leave *Osprey* for *Jollymore*, to become secure enough to convince Albert to persevere, I might still be back in St. Martin with Captain Bligh. This journey was becoming a learning experience, helping me to get in touch with who I was and the of the things that held me back.

The crew from *Stormy Weather* had planned to join the other yacht crews at Curtain Bluff, a nearby resort, to celebrate the winners and trade stories of the day's races. Our group included the skipper Paul, the crew and various friends, such as the young Swede, Philippa, and myself. Curtain Bluff was rather elegant; high walls, a guard at the gate; very impressive. We sat at a big table in the bar area and ordered a round of drinks. Since I knew Cal had no money, I bought his drink. Later, when I checked on him, I found that someone else had bought him a second one. Of course.

As the evening wore on, most of us drifted out behind the resort. I guess the wall, gate and guard were for show or to give resort vacationers a sense of security, because it was totally open in the back to the beach. There we found local vendors cooking and selling food. It smelled wonderful and we were all hungry by then, so we spent much of the night enjoying the native dishes.

We had all arrived at Curtain Bluff by sharing taxis, but by the time we were ready to leave, we were lucky to hitch a ride in the back of a pick up truck that was going to the dockyard. It amazed me how quickly friends were made in the transient world of yachting and how generous people were in helping each other. If you stayed around the islands for long, you met quite a few people and it was great fun when you saw them again on another island. Race Week was like a family reunion for the yachting types who'd been around for a while. As a boat came into the harbor, it was frequently greeted by shouts from other boats. It made it seem like old home week. As one of the employees at Admirals Inn commented, "It is a special time of year, when all of our old friends come back to see us. We enjoy seeing them very much and I think many hate to leave, because when we come to work in the morning after the Admiral's Ball, a few are still there, asleep on the couches."

Races for the next two days were being held on the far side of the island, not visible from shore. Since I would have the use of the dinghy, after I had delivered Albert and Cal to *Stormy Weather*, I thought I would spend the day exploring. Whenever I could, I gave young men rides back and forth from yachts where they crewed. There was a commercial dinghy operating in English harbor, but some didn't have the money to use it. Once ashore, I decided to take a bus to St. John's, the capital of Antigua.

While waiting for the bus, I joined a group of spectators who were watching the Royal Antigua Police Force Band practice for the final festivities at the end of the week. There were twelve men or so, and they looked very fine. Even though they were not military, they had learned a great deal from the British army; uniform, marching, music and expertise. The chap who carried the big bass drum even had on a leopard skin, as seen in the British army.

Meeting Steven

As I started to turn away I was greeted by a tall, young, British lad, who introduced himself as Steven. He asked to borrow a pencil and during our subsequent conversation, it came out that he had managed to get from England to Antigua by crewing on sailboats and was as good as out of money. He was looking for another boat to crew on or for some sort of job. He was extremely thin, but had this wonderful, outgoing way about him. He had been camping out in one of the booths which had recently been erected on the grass to serve as bars for the final night of Race Week. He amazed me. I knew I had never been so resilient, so apparently carefree, not even when I was his age.

The bus ride to St. John's did not take long; the island itself was only fourteen miles long and eleven miles wide. The capital, unlike English Harbor, was small and rather dusty, with evidence of much poverty. Most of the inhabitants were descended from slaves who had worked on sugar plantations. There was one little department store, where I was able to buy an inexpensive pair of shoes to wear to the Lord Nelson Ball. The Ball, held on the last official night of Race Week, was a dressy affair and I was traveling with just the basics in a duffel bag. I would make do with the one outfit I had brought to use for church.

I saw the tall, skinny Brit again, after I got back from St. John's. He had made friends with some of the locals who hung around on the porch outside Limey's bar and he was gathering information about the life and politics of the dockyard. He sounded like he was planning to start a business here. It was the end of the day and an old local woman was packing up the unsold produce from her booth. Steven approached her about buying the ten or twelve remaining bananas. He didn't have the local currency and he set about talking to onlookers and shop owners, trying to exchange the little money he had, for what he needed.

It was marvelous to watch as he involved people in his project. When his mission was accomplished, and he had purchased the bananas, he walked around giving a banana to each person who wanted one. He ended up with two bananas having given away enough to feed himself for several days, talk about the widow's mite in the bible; he was a close second.

Lay Day

It was very pleasant to have Cal aboard *Jollymore*. He was easy-going and much more open to doing things than Albert. After two days of racing, there was a one day break. Those who wished, could attend a day-long event, called Lay Day, held at the Antigua Yacht Club. Albert was not interested, so Cal and I took a commercial dinghy ashore to check it out. I paid the nominal entrance fee and we wandered around and enjoyed watching some very serious partying. Booths had been set up for selling hot dogs, hamburgers and sandwiches. There was a fully equipped bar and plenty of beer, the drink of choice. The games included: tug of war at the water's edge, so that the losing team ended up falling in; rubber raft races with much cheating; a beer drinking contest with contestants who didn't need any more beer; a three legged race with pushing and tripping and finally, the limbo. The games until then had been quite rough and tumble, wild fun, and were mostly played by young men. The limbo was different, and the apparent winner was a lithe and attractive young woman. But then Cal entered the contest and he was amazing to watch. He bent over backwards, until he was barely one foot off the ground and still could move, step by step, under the pole. He won two tickets for dinner at the Galley Restaurant, quite a lovely prize. Cal graciously invited me to share his good fortune.

Late that afternoon, we returned to *Jollymore* and told Albert of our day's adventures and our plans for dinner; he was not pleased. He felt that since Cal had been staying on his boat, he should have been the one invited to dinner. He was probably right and if we had been smarter we would have avoided the disaster that followed. He was most upset and vocal about his displeasure, not wanting anything more to do with us, so Cal and I decided to leave him there and went ashore for our dinner. When we came back later, Albert was drunk and had trashed his boat. He had broken jars of food on the cabin floor and loaded the space up with all kinds of trash. When Albert saw us, he untied his dinghy and went off into the night doing wheelies and narrowly missing nearby yachts. His behavior was a surprise, for he normally drank very little and never on the boat. Cal and I set about cleaning up the mess and I tried to decide what I would do next. That was it with Albert! First he told me how he had put a couple off his boat, even after they had helped him sail across the Atlantic, a big red flag. The second red flag was his show of childish temper after his navigational error, and now this. Cal had to stay on *Jollymore*, because he still had two days of racing with Albert as crew on *Stormy Weather*. Fortunately, I had a friend on a Canadian boat that I felt I could stay with for a few days, so I took a commercial dinghy ashore the next morning. I was finally learning a lesson I badly needed, to let go when things were not right.

Before going to my friend's boat, I went to the ladies bathroom. It was located in the same building as Limey's and was equipped with showers, plenty of free hot water, sinks with real mirrors above them. What joy! But when I walked into the restroom there, sitting on the counter, was a large Rasta man, who had been smoking pot. I looked at him very sternly and said firmly; "This is the ladies restroom and you must leave at once," and he did!. Oh my goodness what a surprise. I was really getting the hang of taking charge of my life.

Finding A New Boat

My next job was to find another boat on which to crew. There were bulletin boards placed in strategic places such as Admirals Inn and Carib Marine, the marine supply and grocery store. The "crew wanted" ads usually gave a destination, an approximate date of departure, the name of boat and the best time to be contacted by VHF. Most yachts kept their radios on at a designated channel, which in Antigua was 68. Once contact was made with the boat, a switch was made to another channel to have a conversation. As I was pursuing the ads, I met Steven once again and he told me he had a job going to the States. We were both very pleased with his success. I looked everywhere hoping to see Cal, but to no avail. I had grown very fond of him and was disappointed at not having the opportunity to say goodbye. Perhaps I would see him later.

My method of finding a boat was to ask around and follow leads. I found that being persistent and not taking the turndowns personally worked best for me. Soon after Race Week ended, all the boats would be leaving. Some would head for the Mediterranean, some to the States or Canada, some down island with Venezuela as their destination, and a few to the United Kingdom. There were beautiful, big charter boats with professional crews who kept everything looking like new; there were boats being delivered by paid captains to a place of the owners choice. Usually these boats took on crew for little or no pay, just an opportunity to get a free ride somewhere. I searched the bulletin board for possibilities. I knew it would not be easy for there were many young men and a few young women living this life of adventure, and I appeared to be the only representative of my age and sex. Approaching a large, square rigger called *Fair Jeannie*, I found the captain had filled his crew, but he gave me a lead. Trying that lead next, I walked up to the boat and requested to speak to the captain. I found he, also, had just filled his crew needs, but he was kind and gave me another lead, and so it went. One of the leads was for a ketch at anchor in Falmouth Harbor. Her name was *Panther*, I tried reaching her by VHF with no luck.

The Lord Nelson Ball

On Friday night, the Lord Nelson Ball was held at Admirals Inn. My Canadian gentleman friend, who was about my age, was my date for the evening. The preparations began early in the day. A canopy of sails was set over the garden terrace, a footbridge was placed over the moat to the dinghy dock and floral decorations adorned the tables. Numerous temporary bars were placed throughout the grounds to accommodate the unlimited free drinks included in the price of the ticket. When the party started at 9:30, everyone arrived dressed in their finest. The men looked dashing in jackets and tie, and the women were elegantly dressed in their best. For me this was my church going dress, enhanced with some jewelry I had just bought locally and my new shoes. The transformation of the salt-stained, wind-blown men, accompanied by their lovely ladies was striking.

Those eighteenth century naval officers of the British fleet would have been surprised and no doubt pleased at the way Nelson's Dockyard was now being used. Here trophies were presented, and the winning yachts were tied in a semi-circle off the Admirals Inn dinghy dock at the waters edge, in the much sought after, floodlit, winners circle. *Stormy Weather* was tied up there. Her skipper, Paul, had racked up quite a few victories this week. The band played and we danced on the terrace in the moonlight. It was hard to believe Admirals Inn was once a sail loft set in the corner of the old naval dockyard, and that the massive pillars, around which we danced, once supported a boathouse roof.

Dockyard Day

Time was running short for me to find a boat and I was getting a little nervous. On Saturday, Dockyard Day, when the final rowdy festivities had begun, I was watching the fun from the porch of Limey's Bar. I had been there for the better part of the afternoon. First, there was the greased pole contest, where young men tried to see how far out over the water they could walk on a pole covered with axle grease. Next, came the homemade boat contest. The rules were, the boat could never previously have been in the water, and it needed a crew of six to move it. One of the more successful competitors, was a boat made of beer kegs lashed together. I think the crew had just drunk the beer shortly before the race, because one of the kegs came unleashed and went floating off in a direction all its own. Right after the frivolity ended, trophies were presented and it was during that ceremony that I noticed a man wearing a sign around his neck: "Crew Wanted to the U.K.." Until now the Mediterranean or Venezuela had been my top choice for a destination, but I quickly decided that England would do fine. The Lord does have a sense of humor; who would have thought the answer to my search for a boat would have been handed to me in such an amusing manner.

By now, I was finding it quite easy to strike up a conversations with complete strangers. I found most people open to talking. Walking up to the man with the sign around his neck, I inquired about his boat. It turned out it was the yacht, *Panther*, anchored in Falmouth Harbor. We introduced ourselves and I learned his name was Conover. He appeared to be an older man, slightly balding and thin, with the weathered look of one who had spent much time in the elements. He was looking for crew to sail to Bermuda, the Azores, and finally his home, Lymington, England. He had one crew member already, but wanted two more. We chatted a bit and set up a plan to get-together the following day, after I had gone to church. He would show me the boat and we'd get to know each other. I ran into Albert later in the day. He was walking with a woman about his age, whom he introduced as his new crew. I wished him well and thanked him for my time as crew on *Jollymore*. He had come into my life in a time of need and I appreciated that.

Life Aboard Panther

Panther was a ketch, a popular rig for midsize cruising boats. A ketch has two masts with the shorter mast located aft, behind the cockpit. At 44 feet, it was the largest boat I had crewed on. To give you an idea of the age of *Panther,* she was used in the evacuation of British Expeditionary Forces in 1940 during WWII. For those too young to remember, the Germans had trapped the British forces in Dunkirk, where their only escape was by sea. Small private fishing boats and yachts were used to get close to shore, ferrying men out to larger vessels. Almost 350,000 men escaped in this manner over a nine day period, until the Germans got too close to continue the evacuation. A piece of equipment from that time was a huge, gray, metal radio box positioned over what would become my bunk in the captain's cabin. In spite of her age and neglected condition, *Panther* was basically a beautiful boat with a teak deck and a large interior cabin of dark varnished wood. She even had two heads. A small forward cabin was filled with extra sails and a door that lead to the second head. The main cabin had benches that could convert to bunks, a table for dining or working, a full galley including a refrigerator, a propane stove with oven and a large sink. There were cabinets for storage, a fully stocked bar and a desk with a radio and global positioning system. Aft, and down several steps, was the captain's cabin with two bunks and a door leading into the other head. *Panther* looked very comfortable, but well worn, like a pair of very old slippers. There was a film of dirt and grease over everything in the galley. There clearly hadn't been a female crew member on this boat for a long time; cleanliness was not a priority.

Conover had been at sea for three years, circumnavigating the globe. He was a retired banker, who had worked in Hong Kong before retiring, and was an old hand at sailing. He had started out using family and friends on his trip around the world, but he had been at sea for so long, he was down to using whatever crew he could find to finish up his voyage. After a short visit, I felt Conover and I got along fine and I liked the idea of having more than one crew member. We came to a meeting of minds, mainly that I had enough sailing experience to be of help and could pay my own way. On his part, he had a great boat, well equipped and he seemed to be sane. Only time will tell on that one. Perhaps the close quarters and the stresses on a sailboat make character problems show up more profoundly and quickly. I agreed to move over to *Panther* the next day.

As I stuffed my duffel bag, I found I had more than I needed. It had been packed with the idea of a six month long voyage to New Zealand, with very few stopping places along the way. I gave away a set of sheets and towels among other things, I was surprised at how little I needed. In this climate one could get by, while on the boat at least, with very little. However, when we were nearer to England, where the weather would be colder, it would be quite another story.

With no plans to leave Antigua for the next few days, I accepted an invitation to go dancing with my Canadian friend. We took a taxi to Shirley Heights, a favorite place to party on Sunday afternoon and evening. Here, on it's high hilltop location, was a ruined building and fortifications that dated from the eighteenth century. At present, the building, in the process of restoration, was not being used except as a backdrop for the party. The location afforded a panoramic view of English and Falmouth harbors and the ocean beyond, and it was quite a magnificent sight, especially later in the day as the sun went down. When we arrived in the afternoon, we found a steel pan band playing in the yard and, for those who were hungry, barbecue being cooked in cut off steel drums. It smelled and tasted mighty good! In the evening, another band took over. On a dance floor of uneven ground, the dancing was as inventive and foolish as one wanted to make it. Loving to dance and with no problem being foolish, we danced for most of the afternoon and evening, with short breaks for libations. It was a joyful way to spend a Sunday. I wouldn't be seeing my Canadian friend again, as he planned to return to Canada and his family. It was hard to say goodbye to such a delightful friend and escort; we had good times together.

The following day I decided to try my hand at boardsailing, also known as windsurfing. Having taken a couple of lessons while in Seattle, where it was just catching on as a sport, I was eager to try my skill. On a beach nearby, just a short distance from where *Panther* was at anchor, I found a place to rent equipment. An enterprising young man had built a shack and set himself up in business with just a few old boards and sails. For those who have never tried this sport, you would find it a great source of merriment to watch a novice trying to stand on the board and get it to head into the desired direction. Due to my classes in Seattle, I did have enough skill to climb on the board, stand up, pull the heavy, awkward sail up out of the water, and hold it until the wind filled the sail, all without falling over. It had taken me several long lessons of continually falling over into the freezing water of Lake Washington to achieve this skill. Very humbling! Having watched others skim over the water at high speed, even lifting into the air at times, with their boards at one with their bodies, I had a great desire to do the same. It would feel like being a bird I was sure. But the surf of the Atlantic ocean made what little skill I had, disappear. Eventually I managed to get up on the board and sail quite a distance from land. I was so thrilled to have finally gotten the darn thing up and going, I didn't want to stop. But, and this was a serious but, there was the problem of turning around, a not so easily learned skill and one I did not have. Trying over and over to turn the board around only to fail; having covered myself with bruises and using up all my energy in my efforts, I was really getting concerned. What if no one saw me out here—getting farther and farther from land? I was starting to wonder how far away the next island might be. I was greatly relieved when a motor boat came to retrieve me and tow me to shore. I should have known the young owner wouldn't want to lose his equipment and destroy his fledgling business.

47

Patrick, a young man from Boston, was our other crew member on the *Panther*. He had been working at the Stock Exchange in N.Y.C., as a commodity broker, when he decided on a lifestyle change. He had been aboard *Panther* for several weeks, agreeing to crew for Conover to England. As the forward cabin was full of sails, he bunked in the main cabin. That left the remaining bunk, located in Conover's cabin, for my use. At first this was disconcerting, but I fell back on my old ploy of sleeping with my large, white bible on my chest, until I found I had no need to worry. Conover wanted to have three crew for the rest of his voyage, but in the end we had to depart from Antigua with just Patrick, me and the skipper.

Back To St. Martin

Conover would be heading in a northerly direction back to the island of St. Martin. I wondered if Don and Peggy would still be there. Conover needed to have some work done on the boat's motor and Philipsburg was noted for it's repair facilities. From there he planned to continue going north to Bermuda, a traditional jumping off place to our next stop, which was east, across the Atlantic ocean to a group of islands off the coast of Portugal, the Azores. The final leg of the journey was to again go north, to the U.K. On the morning of our departure, we motored to English harbor, where we topped off our fuel and water supply and did the paperwork required when leaving any port. Antigua had been an exciting place to be for Race Week and it was hard to see that special time come to an end. But it was a beautiful day for a sail, so off we set for our next destination, St Martin.

Life aboard *Panther* was easy going and most pleasant and at the end of the day, we always had a sundowner from Conover's well stocked bar. He had spent most of his life with the Bank of Hong Kong, and was accustomed to the finer things such as cocktails, good food, wine and beer. He had a refrigerator, so we took turns fixing meals with fresh food and cold drinks. We had a rule while at sea, only one alcoholic beverage a day. That rule was usually broken by noon. We settled into a routine of sharing duties and standing watch in four hour increments. Because there were three of us, the watch during the night hours was not as onerous. Alone on watch, as a Saturday turned into Sunday, I enjoyed my own worship time. I saw the sun come up with the sound of my favorite hymns being played on a tape recorder I had brought with me. The wind had been light and coming from the stern, so the main sail luffed and rattled in it's slides, while the gentle waves slapped against the side of the boat. If heaven was a place where you could do your favorite thing, I thought this would fill the bill.

Everyday, the warm winds blew and, too soon, we had covered the roughly 100 miles to Philipsburg on the island of St. Martin. The trip had been every sailor's dream, downwind sailing, lovely weather, beer in hand, a trip we wished would never end. Philipsburg was back where my journey had started on *Osprey*, a boat with no head, no motor, no radio, an old row boat with misfitting oars and a very difficult man for a skipper. What a change it was to be on *Panther*. I finally saw how dangerous it would have been to sail on *Osprey* to New Zealand and how desperate and foolish I had been. How could I not but think, my guardian angel was watching over me.

We went first to customs, and then the police station, to have our passports stamped and the arrival of the boat registered, and then went in search of a repair facility. Finding what we needed just a short distance down the quay, we got in line to have the engine fixed. It was a handy location: the boat being tied up to cleats located on the sea wall, so we could simply step ashore. This gave us the freedom of coming and going as we pleased. When in harbor, Conover flew a large British flag at the stern of the boat and I was proud to fly a small American flag on a forward spreader, to indicate there was a crew member from the U.S.A. onboard.

It was fun for me to return to a place I knew and I was delighted to have a chance to look up my old friends. I introduced Conover to the parasailing crew, Jim, Nick and Louise and we hired them to take us out on their boat, so Conover could have a trip aloft. The parasail business was doing quite well and another couple went out with us to go air-borne. Patrick had gone his own way, and we did not see him again until we were ready to depart for Bermuda. That left Conover and me to get any chores handled. It was while we were walking through a small park, that I saw Don and Peggy sitting on a bench, watching the world go by. Stopping to chat and introduce Conover, I learned they were looking for a professional skipper to sail *Osprey* through the

Panama Canal and back to Seattle. In my opinion that was not very likely to happen, any professional who took a look at *Osprey* wouldn't want to take the job. They wouldn't be as naive as I was. Giving up on the idea of sailing to New Zealand, the two had donated all the food we spent weeks buying, to a Catholic convent and orphanage. I was glad to hear that. They had visited only two nearby islands before returning to St. Martin, their home-base. I was not at all surprised. Everything on *Osprey* was regimented and disciplined, it was as if Don and Peggy could not start something, unless they knew how it would turn out. In truth, nothing can be certain and nothing remains the same; one must be willing to make it up, to create it anew. However, they were the ones who had started me on this journey and I was forever grateful. If Peggy had not wanted me to come, and Don had not agreed, I would never have been on this voyage.

Once the engine was fixed we did the usual departure procedures, topping off the water and gas, and visiting customs and the police station to check out. Patrick joined us again the day before we were due to sail; I don't know how he figured out the timing.

Map of St. George Harbor, Bermuda

St. George Harbor, Bermuda

Bermuda, about one thousand miles from St. Martin, was our next destination. Again, sailing conditions were ideal and Conover, Patrick and I fell back into our routine of taking turns cooking, cleaning and standing watch. The ten day trip went by all too quickly. As we pulled into St. George Harbor in Bermuda, we recognized many of the yachts that had been with us in Antigua and felt immediately at home. The harbor was crowded with boats, three deep, tied up to the sea wall, right at the edge of the town square. We had to climb over other boats to get to the shore, which turned out to be a way to make new and very interesting friends. Several of the boats were quite small, including one that was twenty-four feet and one that was twenty-seven feet. Their skippers had crossed the Atlantic and would cross again to get home. These were amazingly adventurous people. The twenty-seven foot boat was skippered by a young man by the name of Thomas, from the Isle of Wight in the English channel. He had brought his father along to share in his adventure and I marveled at the enjoyment they had in each other. The twenty-four foot boat was owned by two brothers, looking to be in their early twenties, also from England. Several boats tied up to us were from Canada. The owners sailed to the West Indies, every winter, and then on to Venezuela. This sounded like a splendid idea to me, I was always seeking sunshine and warmth.

I found myself running into people I had gotten to know in other ports. A young woman, Anne, and her little daughter, Sylvie, were coming into a grocery store as I was leaving. We had first met in St Martin and she agreed to join me on *Panther* to visit for a while and chat. Anne had a fascinating story. She had purchased a thirty-five foot boat some years earlier, and Jake, who had been living on it, asked if he could stay on as crew. He fell in love with the lovely, fair-haired Anne and, eventually, he was able to win her hand in marriage. They had been living onboard, anchored in Marigot on St. Martin, where Jake had worked as a carpenter until this trip. Their daughter Sylvie, a totally captivating blonde, blue-eyed nymph of around three years, had spent her life on the thirty-five foot boat. Anne related a story of what life was like aboard a small boat with a baby just learning to crawl. Sylvie had managed to climb up on the deck and fallen overboard. Jake jumped off one side and Anne off the other and they quickley retrieved their baby girl. This event had scared them and they made teaching her to swim their immediate priority. When I saw them, they were on their way to Canada, to visit Jake's parents.

The town where we tied up, St George, was named for the patron saint of England. Founded in 1605, it was Britain's oldest colony in the new world, antedating the Mayflower's landing in Plymouth in 1620. The town was beautiful, so sparkling clean and picture-perfect. The buildings in St. George were all pastels: pinks, yellows, greens and blues. The roofs were white and sparkled in the sunshine. It turned out the roofs were used to collect water, channeled, when it rained, into large cisterns on the sides of the houses. In this island paradise, fresh water was precious. The white roofs made quite a contrast to the brightly colored gardens, lush with a profusion of sweet smelling flowers. The many, narrow streets, more like alleyways, were indicative of the age of the town. The major buildings, like the banks, had flags flying, as did the very British looking pubs and inns. It was charming.

The island of Bermuda had been discovered when a ship from England, bound for the new world, was blown off course in a storm and wrecked on the coast. Salvaging what they could, the sailors built a new, but smaller ship called Deliverance and in 1609 it continued the voyage to what became Jamestown, Virginia. A replica of the ship was on display on Ordinance Island, which had a bridge connecting it to the town square. In the early days of the colony, Ordinance Island was used to store ammunitions for the forts nearby. The town square had a war memorial and cannons of different sizes and it was the location for various forms of entertainment. There were stocks, a whipping pole and a dunking chair used for the reenactment of scenes from colonial times. When a cruise ship arrived, it would tie up to Ordinance Island and costumed players would put on a show for the passengers including being put in the stock or placed in the chair and dunked in the harbor, forms of punishment used in the early days of the town. Can you imagine being dunked in the water, not quite sure if you would be pulled up before you drowned. On some nights there were steel drum bands and Gombey dancers. Gombey dancers, by tradition, were local men who dressed in wild masquerade costumes. The art of the dance was passed down in families and to be a dancer, your father had to have been a dancer. *Panther* was tied up to the sea wall in the town center, so we had a front row seat for all the fun.

One of the delights of the sailing life, was the ease with which you made friends, and our boat soon became a center for social gatherings. We gave it the nick name "The Panther Inn," for we were often in competition with the "White Horse Inn" across the square. The difference, our drinks were free. One of the Gombey dancers had taken to joining us and bringing his five year old son. Their English accents delighted us.

Patrick, who had done his disappearing act and been gone quite a few days, returned one afternoon while Conover was running an errand on shore. He looked terrible and it was hard to ignore the fact that he had been on an alcoholic binge. His disappearance on St. Martin must have been for the same reason. At that time, when he returned to the boat, he'd given most of his money to Conover to hold. It had seemed a little odd, but now I understood why. Patrick told me that he had called home and learned of his grandmother's death. He planned to fly back to Boston. He took the money Conover set aside for him, packed his bag, and he said goodbye and left. He was a very attractive young man, an enjoyable companion and had been in control of his illness while on the boat. Perhaps he had hoped that by being on a boat, he could stop binge drinking, but alas there was always a port. I was extremely sorry to see him go.

O C E A N

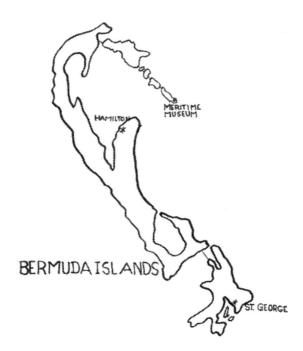

MARITIME
MUSEUM

HAMILTON

BERMUDA ISLANDS

ST. GEORGE

Map of Bermuda

Exploring Bermuda

Conover felt we needed at least three people to sail to England, so it looked like we might be in Bermuda a while looking for another crew member. It was a eureka moment when I found a place to rent a moped and had the freedom to explore the island. The main city, Hamilton, had some very inviting shops, giving me an opportunity to buy warmer clothes for the trip ahead and satisfy my love of shopping. Conover was amused at some of the terms I used. I had bought suspenders to hold up my slightly too big, new pants and he explained in England, suspenders were used for holding up socks and that pants were men's underpants. When I expressed a wish that I had my down vest with me, he informed me a vest is a man's undershirt. When I asked for a flashlight one night, he told me it was called a torch. In time, I'm sure he would find other words to share with me.

Conover joined me, along with Thomas from the Isle of Wight and his father, and we rode mopeds to the far western edge of the island to visit a Maritime Museum. What started out as a beautiful, sunny day ended up with a cold, hard, wind-driven rain that hit us head-on for the 22 mile long trip home. Not fun on a moped. Being cold to the bone, I retired to my bunk to bury myself under anything that might warm me. Conover, a kind and thoughtful person, brought me a drink, but it was my favorite drink for hot days, a gin and tonic with plenty of ice. He clearly did not understand "cold to the bone." In spite of the miserable trip back, the visit to the Bermuda Maritime Museum had been enjoyable. The museum was described as "A Walk Back In Time." For more than half a century, starting in 1809, the British Admiralty had been building a naval station that was to be the Royal Navy's premiere base in the Western Atlantic, "The Gibraltar of the West." The base encompassed twenty-five acres including the fortress, marine engineering works, administrative outpost of empire and a parade ground dominated by a ten foot tall figurehead of King Neptune, which had once graced the bow of a British ship. Before starting back, we had all bought lunch from a small restaurant in, what had been, the boat loft. We sat in the sunshine on the patio, enjoying the view. Being a history buff, I had enjoyed this outing, as I did all of Bermuda.

Meeting Scott

As boats and friends came and went, we remained, looking for another crew member. Soon, what had been a teeming harbor, was reduced to just a few boats and the weekly cruise ship. I struck up a friendship with a tall, blue-eyed young man in his late twenties; I had found a kindred, adventurous soul. Scott came from a very wealthy family in the southern U.S., where his father owned a newspaper. His twin brother was in the family business, but Scott had opted for the less conventional life of crewing on a sailboat. The boat he was on was docked in Hamilton, where he was helping the owners, a middle-aged couple, sail across the Atlantic. Together, Scott and I devised a game. Once a day one of us would challenge the other to do something slightly outrageous. I had the advantage. Because of my age and sex, most people assumed I was harmless. Scott, because of his age and sex, was more suspect. Our first challenge was to walk through a posh hotel lobby, out to the pool in the back, swim, shower and use their towels. The following day, since we had accomplished that without incident, we decided we would board the cruse ship tied-up on nearby Ordnance Island, and see how far we could get. Walking right past security as though I belonged, I was starting up the grand staircase when I saw that Scott had been stopped by the guards and denied entrance. There are times when old age and cunning win out over youth and strength.

Special to this island paradise were the number of fortifications; some had become tourist attractions, but most were just places on the shore to discover quite by accident. There were beautiful views all over the island and one day climbing the rocks for the view, I discovered a completely sheltered beach far below. It would be ideal for small children. My personal favorite was Horseshoe Bay Beach, where I could buy two dollar hamburgers and view the aqua-colored fish in the water. The shopping in Hamilton was great, especially if followed by lunch at the Bermuda Yacht Club. The Dinghy Club shower and bar, Whoopie the bartender, dinghy racing, rafting up, and the friendliness of the people were other things that I found made this island so delightful.

The weeks slipped by and we still had not found suitable crew. One man looked somewhat promising, and said he wanted to return home to England, to his wife and children. However on the day appointed for him to join us, he did not show up. Apparently the draw of home and family was not enough to outweigh living in Bermuda. With hurricane season soon to be upon us, Conover and I finally decided if this was the caliber of the person we might get, we should sail one hand short. I turned in my moped and said goodbye to friends. I had really enjoyed my time in Bermuda. Even though I hated to leave, I felt very fortunate to be crewing with Conover as skipper; I had finally found a winner. As we were waiting to clear customs and leave port we ran into Paul, of *Stormy Weather* fame. He was just arriving in Bermuda; destination Horta in the Azores, the first stopping place for us and for most boats crossing the Atlantic. Maybe we would see him there and share a drink together.

Next Stop The Azores

After leaving port in Bermuda I requested that Conover teach me how to navigate with a sextant. Although he had satellite navigation or GPS on the boat, which could do everything with only a little programing, I thought it would be fun to learn to do without it. So with the exception of the first few days, we had it turned off. Every day we took a morning and noon sighting with the sextant and worked out our position. Conover worked out our position that is, I couldn't even find what ocean I was on and soon cried out for relief. Conover worked diligently with me for hours each day, but I was never able to get it and finally realized this was something I probably could never learn. Besides the satellite navigation, another handy piece of equipment on board, was a device that adjusted the tiller automatically when there was a slight change in wind direction. Conover called it George and it was a huge help at night, when on watch.

Sailing north by northeast to take advantage of the gulf stream, we were soon well settled into a routine. Taking turns every four hours, I took the ten to two watch at night and was again on watch at six in the morning. At night, I always wore the harness that my son-in-law, Bob gave me, attached to the lifeline on the boat. Unless we were in calm waters, I wore a life vest and foul weather gear. We often had rain squalls that would come through at night and I had learned to walk in a crouching position when on deck, always looking for my next hand hold. When cold or tired of standing, I checked for any boat traffic, turned on George in case of a change in wind direction and went below to the cabin for shelter, keeping the bad weather out by closing up most of the hatchway. I checked every ten minutes or so for my course heading and for ships on the horizon. We had seen no other boats, except for two freighters. We contacted one, the *Margaret Lykes,* on the VHF to acknowledge our existence, get current weather conditions, and check on our position. Some days later, we passed the second ship, *Sealane Commitment*. It was late at night and I asked Conover to contact her just to hear another voice. It was interesting how important it was for me to know someone was out there with us. Longfellow expressed my thoughts when he wrote;

> "Ships that pass in the night,
> and speak to each other in passing;
> Only a look and a voice,
> then darkness again and a silence"

The watch at six in the morning was my favorite. For a few days, I had seen the sun dead ahead of *Panther,* peeking over the horizon at the water's edge, slowly rising, until it dominated the sky with its brilliance. A pathway of light was created by the sun's reflection on the water and we sailed down that glorious, golden pathway. What a gift; such stunning beauty! There was no other sign of life, except for the sailing jellyfish that frequented these waters and an occasional bird. The birds looked so lonely and caused me to wonder how they could survive so many hundreds of miles from any land. The jellyfish were plentiful and were of a type I had also seen in Bermuda. They carried a small portion of their bodies like a little coxcomb on the water surface, so that it served to act like a sail. Thus their names, sailing jellyfish. They were blue in color with a slight touch of purple along the outer edge of their sail. One hit me when I was swimming at Horseshoe Bay Beach in Bermuda, and it packed a painful sting that lasted for hours.

For some time we had been experiencing downwind sailing, with rough following seas. The boat would glide down a wave and, upon reaching the bottom, lurch and crash, and then start up to repeat the process all over. It seemed each successive wave was larger, until with a final loud crash, the boat shook itself and started up again only to repeat itself. I found the simplest things took great patience and endurance to accomplish, particularly at meal times or for any simple chore that required two hands. A thing like putting on my pants, excuse me, "trousers," had become fraught with danger. It was hard to keep my balance, with two arms and one leg engaged in the business of pulling on the trousers. Opening a cabinet door was an invitation to disaster with canned, or the Brits would say tinned, foods falling out in disarray. It was a relief when we had a change in the weather and the seas calmed.

George Dies

George, which adjusted the tiller automatically, died and it was like losing a crew member. When George had been working, I could go below and fix a cup of coffee, slide the hatch closed if it was cold, read a little or just move around. Now four hours of standing at the wheel was so tedious that I was falling asleep standing up, only to awaken when the sails started luffing, making a loud banging sound against the mast. By then, I was so off course that we were sailing in a circle. It was a cold, tedious, monotonous job and, although I tried to think of different ways to keep myself awake and alert, like singing, trying for interesting thoughts, even moving about a bit with one hand on the wheel, nothing helped. Now my last hour on watch had become a struggle just to stay conscious, let alone stay on course and finally, as a matter of safety, I requested that my watch at night be reduced to three hours. Fortunately that was agreeable with Conover.

We caught a skipjack tuna one day, weighing around five pounds. We had put our fishing line out when we left Bermuda, but we never really expected to catch anything; it was just part of the routine when leaving port. The fish was a welcome treat and as it was my night to cook, I thought a bottle of white wine for dinner would be in order. It had been a good day for sailing, with the boat bounding along on a broad reach, throwing up cascades of water on either side of the bow, as she dipped into the back of the waves. We were joined by twenty or more dolphins, who for a while, cavorted beside our boat. They would swim a little distance, then in groups of four or five, arch and lift their bodies through the air. One fellow had us laughing, as he tried to do a flip while leaping in the air.

We had an easy time for a few days. We were able to keep a magnetic heading of about 100 degrees, with winds fairly constant at about twenty knots, dropping off in the late afternoon and picking up again at night. We were sailing downwind with two jibs, one on either side of the bow in a configuration called wing-on-wing. This was one of my favorite positions to sail, as I liked the challenge of keeping both sails equally filled and pulling. We were still enjoying the fish we had caught; it had a marvelous flavor and firm texture. We were eating on deck in the evenings, putting on a music tape for atmosphere, while we had our sundowner and dinner. The skipper had a very eclectic taste in music and we listened to anything from popular tunes of the forties, to bagpipes from Scotland, to Ella Fitzgerald and Duke Ellington. We were in hopes of seeing the Isle of Flores, one of the Portuguese islands, sometime that night, if the wind held.

Instead the wind dropped and we managed about two knots due to the effects of the Gulf Stream, the only thing moving us forward. So much for seeing the Isle of Flores. In these conditions, we would normally have used the motor, but the engine was overheating, and Conover had taken it apart. They had not done a very good job of fixing it in St Martin. To have access to the engine, part of the floor in the main cabin near the galley had to be lifted up, and as Conover worked on it, his hands became covered with grease. He paid little attention to this and now I understood why, when I had first come aboard *Panther*, things had been black with what I thought was dirt, but really was engine grease.

Big wrinkles festooned the sails, which were making a noise as they flapped about, beating against the standing rigging, abetted by the pounding of a short, choppy sea. We finally took them down to avoid damage caused by the flogging of the sails and to relieve our brains of the constant noise. Conover went over the side to see if there was any blockage of the engine water exhaust. This was not the problem and he was running out of ideas. The weather was mild and with nothing better to do, we took turns bathing while standing on the bow of the boat, first using salt water, then rinsing with fresh. We had a hundred-gallon tank of water that we hadn't touched yet.

The evening was quite clear and we again had dinner on deck so we could enjoy the sunset. Conover had made stew with tinned meat; quite good. We were running out of Conover's wonderful homemade bread. I would have made more, but it was impossible to move around below deck with the spread-out engine project. We had used all our fresh food except for eggs, which I had preserved by coating each one with Vaseline, a trick I had learned from a book on cruising. At night, when it was quite dark, we could see lovely streaks of phosphorus under the water. I found myself being mesmerized by the movement of the light below. The mood was spoiled when we saw in the distance a yellow pinpoint of light, and soon a yacht came into view on our stern, and slowly motored past us and over the horizon.

Even though the sails were down, we needed to keep an eye out for other boats, primarily ships that might not see us. In the early dawn, when it was my turn to go on watch, we put the sails back up. At first we had a flat sea, but then we got a slight breeze. I was treated to a contrail from a plane overhead that caught the early light. Then some birds circled our boat and I was surprised by the sound of their chirping. Later, the porpoises came again, some of them quite large. They surfaced for air in perfect unison, ballet-like. My watch was spent trying to catch whatever elusive wind there was, which, after several hours of concentrating on the sail and adjusting for every little wind change, was exhausting and nerve wracking.

Sighting The Island Of Flores

Shortly after I turned the watch over to Conover, he sighted land. The first of the Azores Islands was off our port bow. To me it looked like a low lying cloud, but a check on our radio direction finder confirmed it was land. The wind had freshened a bit and we hoped to finally pass Flores that night and reach the island of Faial and the harbor at Horta the next day. But that didn't happen. We were both eager to have this trip over, I know I was, we were making such slow progress and being on watch so often was wearing me down. Conover had lent me some books to help pass the time and one, published by the Cruising Association, had a system whereby one could advertise either for crew or be crew. I told myself to keep that in mind. The second, "The Flying Fish" by the Ocean Cruising Club, was a way to keep track of old friends and have a contact person in places in the world that were popular harbors. The membership was restricted to people who had made one continuous voyage of a thousand miles or more. It seemed I was eligible for membership. Going through the journal, I found that the contact person for Annapolis, Maryland was Judy Wentworth, a next door neighbor of my family on Gibson Island. Another small world discovery.

It was two days since we first sighted Flores! It seemed to take forever after you once sighted land, before you reached it. I had the beacon light and, what looked like a row of other identifying lights, well within sight as I turned in after my six to ten evening watch. Coming up on deck for my next watch, the island didn't appear to be any closer. We were flying a jib called the ghoster, a term Conover used for a very light weight sail and a main sail made of light fabric. The ghoster was able to pick up a whisper of a breeze. I had been on watch for a short time, when the wind picked up and as a new dawn broke, we finally slipped past Flores. The porpoise were out in great numbers, just a few came over to play around the boat. There must have been a school of fish nearby, for the sky was filled with birds. One type of bird, the Shirwaters, had been with us the whole trip, gliding effortlessly for long distances just a few inches above the wave tops. They were now joined by a variety of other birds, who needed the proximity of land to survive. What a pleasure to hear the rush of water under the boat and the wind in the rigging, Next stop: Faial Island and the harbor at Horta!

Island Of Faial

Well, the beckoning lights I mentioned in the prologue of my story disappeared, as the weather changed. We approached the island of Faial early on a cold, misty morning and then we went the wrong way and sailed all around the island before reaching the harbor at Horta, in the late afternoon. To say we were both very tired is an understatement; our brains weren't functioning very well. With no motor, we had to come in under sail and Conover kept vacillating between using the main sail or the jib. At the last minute he decided on the main and we came in too fast, making a crash landing at the cement pier. Fortunately, a young man standing on the harbor wall helped fend us off. Dropping our fenders, we tied up to nearby cleats, checked in at the customs dock, and were assigned a slip. We could hardly wait to sleep though an entire night. We had been at sea for nineteen days, had traveled roughly 1,900 miles or more from Bermuda, and it was a joy and a relief to be in port.

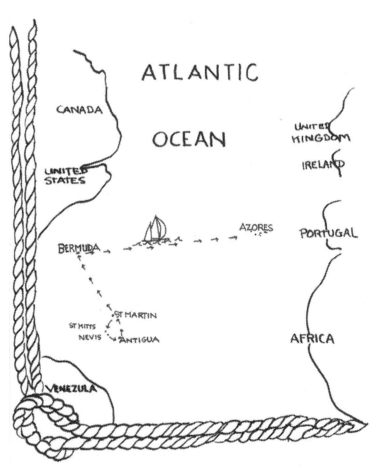

Map of the journey across the Atlantic.

The facilities in Horta were first class. There was a space for us to tie up our 44ft. ketch at a floating pier, complete with connections for electricity and water. At the hub of this village of boats, was a new building that housed showers with plenty of hot water, phones, washers, dryers and a large message board. Oh the joy of it, all the services that can make life ashore so pleasant. Reading the message board was something I had learned to do early on when I reached a new harbor. It made me feel slightly more educated about my surroundings. There were the usual ads for boating equipment, sail and electric repair, letters from boats that had passed through, for friends who were due to follow and the always intriguing notices of crew wanted. It was good to be ashore.

Our next door neighbors on the dock were a couple we knew from Bermuda and it was fun to see them again. It was a treat for me to have a woman to talk to, we seem to speak a different language, a language that I had missed. We traded books which I treasured, as they helped relieve the tedious times. Since we were in Portuguese territory now, it wouldn't be easy to find books in English and I had long since read all that Conover had. After enjoying a good shower, we worked on the boat, draping the sails everywhere so they could dry in the sun before we folded them and stored them in the forward cabin. Conover went off to find someone to repair the engine and I went to town to provision our empty larder. It was good to be ashore, or did I already say that?

Horta had a perfect harbor and was a favorite stopping off place for boats of all sizes. They came here to rest up and provision before taking off for places like England, the Mediterranean and the U.S. The town itself was not very large and the few bars and restaurants were crowded and noisy, filled with happy sailors. Very popular was Peter Azevedo "Cafe Sport," where the people sat at tables jammed together—so crowded they spilled out onto a deck. Surrounding the docking area were high cement walls which had become a canvas for a wonderful collage of paintings and names of boats that had passed through. It was quite a treat to walk around and view this little piece of history. One that was especially poignant, was a painting of a tall ship, the Marques, dated 1982. Underneath, was printed "Lost at sea, may she and the 19 who went with her rest in peace." I decided to add *Panther* to the wall art and walked into town to buy some small cans of paint. I painted a large red background and then a black panther, with the name of our boat, and the date we had arrived.

There were many mega-yachts in the harbor; some were quite famous like Adnan Khashoggi's 282-foot *Nabila* and Donald Trump's *Octopussy*. Off on a far dock, was the super yacht *Christina*, owned by Aristotle Onassis, husband of Jacqueline Kennedy Onassis. It caused much stir due to being the last word in opulence, and also because of the owner's famous wife. I made friends with a captain of one of the less prestigious yachts and was invited aboard. Even the crew quarters were luxurious. The crew lived aboard full-time and took the yacht to wherever the owners wanted to meet it. Quite a nice life, I think.

My adventurous young friend, Scott, showed up in Horta and we resumed hanging out. He was very good-looking and great company; too bad I was old enough to be his mother. His dream was to own his own boat and some months later, when I was back in Seattle, I got a letter asking if I would like to crew for him. His dream of owning his own boat had came true, but by then I had moved on to trying my hand at wind surfing in Baja, Mexico..

Taking advantage of the time available while waiting for the motor to be fixed, I enjoyed hiking the hills around Horta. The land was covered with luxuriant vegetation, particularly hydrangeas, which lined the roadways and helped hedge different pastures. Faial was called the blue island because of the profusion of blue hydrangeas. Horta itself had lush gardens and a coastal esplanade, it was extremely picturesque. Occasionally, there would be a windmill on a hill or a simple religious shrine beside the road. Most of the houses were whitewashed white and whitewashed again and again, which gave them a luminous look in the sunlight. There was a fort in town, Fort of Santa Cruz, which dated from the 16th century and overlooked the harbor. All of the islands in the Azores have a maritime, mild climate owing to the influence of the Gulf Stream.

Our days in Horta passed quickly and within a week the engine was repaired; it was time to continue our journey to England. Conover needed another crew member for the rest of the trip to comply with the particulars of his insurance policy, so he had called home and arranged for his teenage son to join us. We had everything shipshape for a early morning departure and Conover went to the airport to pick up his son. Apparently Conover was much younger than I, if he had a teenaged son. His sun-toughened face and receding hair had me fooled.

While Conover was gone it started to rain, so I quickly gathered up the cushions in the cockpit and made for the ladder leading to the cabin below. Slipping on a rung, I fell and slammed my ribs against a cabinet at the bottom. The pain was excruciating and I realized I needed medical help. Taking a taxi to the hospital in town, I lucked out and got a doctor who spoke English; he had done his internship in the United States. He said my ribs were broken and there was nothing I could do except tough it out.

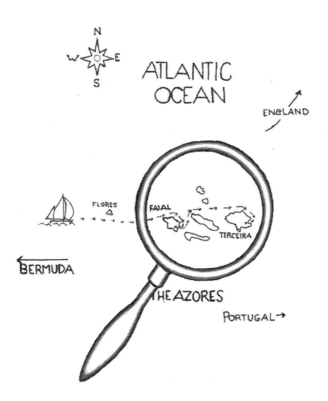

Map of the Islands of the Azores

My Final Journey

Conover still needed me for insurance purposes, even though I was of no use to him as a crew member. We came to an agreement, I would sail with him if he would put me off on the nearest island, if I found I couldn't stand the pain from my ribs. So we sailed away from Faial under an overcast sky, much like the one we had when we first arrived. I found that if I jammed myself into the corner on a bench in the main cabin, I could tolerate the rocking motion of the boat. Lying down that night was bearable but getting up was a miserable, no good, painful experience. Any movement on my part caused excruciating pain, not something you would want to inflict on yourself. Later that day when we caught sight of an island, I asked to be put ashore and Conover kindly complied. We were sailing into a small bay with houses dotting the shore line and looking for a docking area, when we were confronted by a military vessel coming toward us at top speed. It seemed we had wandered into a restricted area and were being stopped by uniformed men with guns. It was a great relief to see it was the U.S. military who were stopping us. What on earth were they doing here and why was this a restricted area were the thoughts that went through my mind. Fortunately I had a military ID card as my former spouse had been in the Air Force. My card worked like a charm. They were willing to take me ashore and let *Panther* go on its way. Having to say a quick goodbye didn't leave any time to feel sad about leaving *Panther* and Conover, it was only later that I experienced my loss. What a grand time we had, a time to remember forever and ever and then some more! What an incredible experience! Once again I felt watched over.

On the shore was a small hotel with a dock and I was dropped off there. Since the waterfront was in a restricted area, there were few other guests and I easily got a room. It turned out that this was the charming town of Praia De Vitoria on the island of Terceira. The U.S. Air Force had a military base there; thus the security we encountered. The island was sixty miles from Faial and we had sailed right past two islands which I had not seen, only to arrive at the one island that had a large airport. and quite a few people who spoke English. Hmm, interesting!

There was little for me to do, except rest and read the only two books I had. The gentleman on the desk at the hotel was very sympathetic to my plight and agreed to help me find a flight that I could take back to the U.S. After about five days, I was well enough to take long walks and adventure started calling me, "come play, come play." Hearing about a bull fight, where locals taunted and ran from the bulls, I found I had a great desire to be part of it all. So off I went on a bus to the town of Angra Do Heroismo, the capital of Terceira. Discovered in the 15th century, Terceira was the third island to be discovered in the Azores, thus it's name. The capital was located on a plateau overlooking the ocean and a large harbor far below. I recognized my friend Scott in the distance and other sailing folks, and I began to wish I could check the message board one more time. But alas, this was to be the end of my sailing saga, something I hated to see end.

When I got back to the hotel, the gentleman at the front desk announced he had found a charter flight that would be landing to refuel on Terceira and he had booked a place for me. With no one to say goodbye to except the gentleman at the desk, I took a taxi to the airport and embarked on my journey home. The flight landed first in New York, just long enough to refuel before flying on to Los Angeles. From there I caught a flight to Seattle. It surprised me how quickly it was all over. Looking back on the roughly two month journey, the pluses and minuses, the good parts and otherwise, I realized what a fabulous and life-changing adventure it had been. What a wonderful gift.

Some time after arriving home, I received a letter from Conover. It seemed he and his son had encountered a terrible storm before they reached England. *Panther* had been knocked about and almost capsized before righting herself. I could just picture Conover's liquor bottles, which he always kept out, all over the cabin. Conover said he was very glad I had gotten off the boat. So was I. What had seemed so negative, with my injured ribs, turned out to be positive. Albert Einstein, one of the greatest minds of our time, said there are two ways to live your life. One is as though nothing is a miracle. The other, is as though everything is a miracle. To me the second way was obvious and it had been borne out over and over throughout my journey.

Putting myself out on the skinny branches of life had been very rewarding. I was tempted to stay in my comfort zone, to stay in the safety of the way things had always been. But then think of all the fun I would have missed, the incredible places I wouldn't have seen, the special people I wouldn't have met and the wonderful memories that will last me a lifetime that I wouldn't have. Someday, I like to think, I might go down to the nearby marina at the Seattle Yacht Club and check out their message board for one more adventure.

Sailing Terms

Burgee, a very small flag used on a sailboat to designate a yacht club or a county.

Bow, front section of the boat.

Broad reach, sailing with the wind over the rear corner of the boat.

Cleat, a fitting around which a line is secured.

Cockpit, open part of the boat.

Companionway, the entrance area and steps from the cockpit into a sailboat's cabin.

Dinghy, a type of small row or powered craft. Taken along when cruising on a larger boat.

Fender, a bumper hung alongside to prevent the hull from rubbing on a dock or other structure.

Galley, a kitchen.

GPS, a world wide navigational system using orbiting satellites.

Hatch, a sliding cover.

Head, the bathroom on a boat or the forward part of the boat.

Jib, the triangular sail attached to the forestay, the front sail on boats with two or more sails.

Ketch, a type of sailboat with two masts.

Knots, a measure of speed equal to one nautical mile or 6075 feet per hour.

Lifeline, a line or wire all around the boat, held up with stanchions, to prevent falling overboard.

Line, a piece of rope used on a boat.

Luffing, the sails waving back and forth.

Mainsail, a sail attached to and behind the main mast.

Mizzen, smaller mast on a ketch or yawl.

Port, the left side of a boat when facing forward.

Quay, the concrete structure at the edge of the water where boats can tie up.

Slip, a berth for a boat in a marina.

Starboard, the right side of a boat when facing forward.

Stern to, to be tied to the dock by the stern or back of the boat.

Tether, a short line or strap that runs between a safety harness and a point of attachment on the boat to prevent going overboard.

VHF radio, very high frequency for ship communication.

Printed in the United States
By Bookmasters